# The Ultimate Guide To Antiques

*How To Find The Best Antiques and Sell For Best Price*

**George K.**

## Table of Contents

Introduction

Chapter 1: Antiques & Antiquing

Chapter 2: Types of Antiques

Chapter 3: Notable Antiques & Antique Experts

Chapter 4: Hunting Antiques

Chapter 5: Earning Bucks from Antiquing

Chapter 6: Taking Care of Antiques

Chapter 7: How to Acquire the Best Antiques at a Great Price

Conclusion

# Introduction

I want to thank you and congratulate you for purchasing the book, *"The Ultimate Guide To Antiques: How To Find The Best Antiques and Sell For Best Price"*.

This book contains proven steps and strategies on how to find valuable Antiques and sell them for a good price.

What are the different classifications of antiques? How do I classify them according to time period? Where do I hunt for antiques? How do I handle this particular type of antique? How do I know this is authentic? How do I know the age of this particular antique? What are the most notable antique collections? What should be the price range for this? How do I handle possible buyers? This book will answer these kinds of questions.

Thanks again for purchasing this book, I hope you enjoy it!

© Copyright 2014 by George K - All rights reserved.

This document is geared towards providing exact and reliable information in regards to the topic and issue covered. The publication is sold with the idea that the publisher is not required to render accounting, officially permitted, or otherwise, qualified services. If advice is necessary, legal or professional, a practiced individual in the profession should be ordered.

- From a Declaration of Principles which was accepted and approved equally by a Committee of the American Bar Association and a Committee of Publishers and Associations.

In no way is it legal to reproduce, duplicate, or transmit any part of this document in either electronic means or in printed format. Recording of this publication is strictly prohibited and any storage of this document is not allowed unless with written permission from the publisher. All rights reserved.

The information provided herein is stated to be truthful and consistent, in that any liability, in terms of inattention or otherwise, by any usage or abuse of any policies, processes, or directions contained within is the solitary and utter responsibility of the recipient reader. Under no circumstances will any legal responsibility or blame be held against the publisher for any reparation, damages, or monetary loss due to the information herein, either directly or indirectly.

Respective authors own all copyrights not held by the publisher.

The information herein is offered for informational purposes solely, and is universal as so. The presentation of the information is without contract or any type of guarantee assurance.

The trademarks that are used are without any consent, and the publication of the trademark is without permission or backing by the trademark owner. All trademarks and brands within this book are for clarifying purposes only and are the owned by the owners themselves, not affiliated with this document.

# Chapter 1: Antiques & Antiquing

By definition, an antique is a work of art created during earlier times. What makes it desirable and valuable are its age, beauty, scarcity, creator, nostalgic quality, and any other unique features. On the other hand, Antiquing is an activity wherein the person involved is shopping, identifying, negotiating, or bargaining for antiques and sometimes, selling them for a higher price.

The usual hubs for antiquing are as follows: garage sales, estate sales, antique districts, collectives, resort towns, and international auction houses. An antiquarian is the person who collects and studies antiques and collectibles.

Many antique enthusiasts have valued these "things of the past" so much that they also engage in activities like primitive decoration and antique restoration.

## Primitive Decorating

Primitive decorating is a style of interior design that reflects early Americana. The usual components of primitive decorating are muted colors with a simplistic but sophisticated look in them. In primitive decorating, you can either utilize antiques or simply incorporate contemporary folk art into the overall design. Contemporary folk art includes objects whose designs have primitive looks but are created using new materials. Examples of this particular genre are objects like paintings, tea cups or tea pots that contain new materials but are made to have a slightly worn or aged look. It is also called country style. Based on the term "country style", it can also be deduced that it's influenced by the art of the mid-1700s and early 1800s.

The recurring common element of primitive decorating are the following: barn stars, crows, willow trees, rag dolls, primitive wooden signs, pottery, and angels.

## Antique Restoration

On the other hand, antique restoration is characterized by either "restoration" of an antique to make it good as new or "conservation" of an antique to prevent further damage and deterioration. Restoration can be as simple as cleaning dirt or grime off a painting, but it can be as complicated as completely rebuilding every part and image.

The usual goal is to prepare the piece either for sale or for purely sentimental reasons, restoring its appearance and functionality. For example, if you are restoring an antique automobile, you have to make it functional for driving. If you want to restore a painting, you have to make it look new again. What makes restoring different from repairing is that if you repair an item, your sole purpose is to restore its functionality.

On the other hand, if you want to restore an item, its original patination should remain. In restoration, the antique collector (or someone who wants the antique to be restored) should also be concerned about the quality of the restoration and the credibility of the restorer because the "over-restoration" of the piece might reduce its aesthetic value. The value of a piece should increase after its restoration. The responsibility of preserving the artwork for future generation lies on the conservators.

Some breakthroughs in restoration are the following: The oldest audio recording from 1878, which was one of the first recordings made on Thomas Edison's phonograph. They preserved and recreated the sound. Another breakthrough is the restoration of a 96-year old American car by the Toyota Automobile Museum in Nagakute, Aichi Prefecture.

There are different terminologies used in the science of antique restoration. They are: conservation, finish restoration, preservation, refinishing, repair, restoration, stripping and salvage.

In conserving an antique, the key is to make sure that the pieces go back as closely as possible to their original condition and appearance. There are two simple guidelines that the Conservation of Cultural Heritage applies in all circumstances: (1) minimal intervention, (2) appropriate materials and reversible methods, (3) full documentation of all work undertaken. The purpose of reversibility is to reduce problems with future treatment. The process must be as detail-oriented as possible.

In brainstorming for the process that the piece must undergo, they must consider the stakeholders involved, the value of the work (both the market value and the sentimental value), and the physical needs of the piece. Details must be paid attention to because one mistake could alter the market value of an antique. An example of an antique undergoing conservation is the painting of a priest in the Church of Secevita Monastery in Romania. The adherent surface deposits, such as dust, were removed using cotton swabs.

Many antique paintings are extremely sensitive to outside conditions such as humidity, light (sunlight and/or artificial sources of light), temperature, and ultraviolet rays. They are usually placed in an artificially-controlled environment wherein these variables are kept in their optimum or safe levels. For example, watercolor paintings should not be exposed to sunlight because pigments might fade. Conservators use equipments such as spectrometers, X-Rays, and microscopes to better analyze the pieces and their components. Moreover, conservationists should also have a background in fields such as chemistry, biology, fine arts, archeology, and anthropology in order to protect the artistic integrity of what they are working on.

On the other hand, the finish restoration is the final process of bringing the piece back to life. It typically involves re-emulsifying the piece by using varnish or shellac. Usually 85% of the original finish remains. The greater the percentage of the original finish kept intact, the greater the piece's market value.

Preservation refers to the process of slowing the deterioration of an antique but it does not involve going through the actual restoration process. It typically involves prevention of further oxidation of wood, etc.

Refinishing involves repairing or removing the wood or finish and applying a new one. As much as possible, this should be the last resort because it destroys significant portions of its antique value. Refinishing not only involves wood, it could also involve other materials such as metal, glass, paint, and plastic.

Repair involves replacement of some physical part of the original piece. The new materials that were added could be altered to look aged but the goal is to keep as much of the original intact.

Stripping involves dipping the piece in chemicals that would remove the paint, patina, and even the glue that holds everything together. As much as possible, this should not be done because it would also be stripped of its value.

Salvage refers to the reuse of bad old pieces as a source of amber, wood, pewter, or ivory. It is basically recycling the material and using it to create another.

## China

When it comes to antiques, the Chinese people usually come to mind. They put high value and importance in their national heritage by protecting Chinese Antiques. The Chinese government utilized the "red chop" mechanism wherein the next owner will place a chop on the antique. These way experts would be able to identify the previous owners of the antique. The chop is simply a piece of red sealing wax. Also, a piece usually bears the "government chop" to verify when it was made.

# Chapter 2: Types of Antiques

If you want to achieve success in buying and selling antiques, you should know which is which. While that might seem simple enough, you mustn't overlook the fact that there are different ways of classifying antique pieces. One could classify them according to their time period or age. They can also be classified according to the cultural era where they came from, or based on their designs and aesthetic value.

**Political History**

First let us classify them according on their political histories. In this book, we will briefly discuss the countries with most eventful royal and political histories such as Britain, France, China, Japan, Italy, and United States.

- ❖ British antiques can be classified according to these historical periods: Medieval (5th to 15th century), Gothic (late medieval period), Elizabethan (1558–1603), Jacobean (1567–1625),

Restoration (1660-1785), William and Mary (1689–1702), Queen Anne (1730–1760), Georgian (1714–1830), Early Victorian (1830 – 1848), Mid-Victorian (1851 – 1867), Late Victorian (1850 – 1910), Modernist (1900 – 1965) and Art Deco (1920-1930s). An example of an antique in the 10th to 12th century (medieval era) is the rare European conical helmet which presently costs 14,000 dollars.

❖ French antiques, such as furniture and decorative objects, can be classified according to their historical periods: Middle Ages (5th to 15th century), Renaissance (14th to the 17th century), Louis XIII (1223 to 1226), Louis XIV (1643 – 1715), Regence ( 1715 - 1723), Louis XV (1715 – 1730), Louis XVI (1774 – 1793), Directoire (1789-1804), Empire (1800–1815), Restoration (1660–1685), Louis Philippe (1830 – 1848), Second Empire (1852–1870), Art Nouveau

(1890–1910), and Art Deco (1920-1930s).

❖ Chinese antiques can be classified according to the following periods: Neolithic (began in the 10th millennium BC), Xia (21st - 17th century BC), Shang (1600 to 1050 BCE), Zhou ( 1046–256 BC), Han (206 BC – 220 AD), Sui period (581–618 AD) , Tang (618–907 AD), Song (960-1127), Jin (265–420), Yuan (1271-1368), Ming (1368–1644), and Qing (1644-1911).

**Pottery, Ceramics, & Porcelain Antique**

Classification of porcelain antique can be divided into five (according to century): Ancient, 17th Century, 18th Century, 19th Century, and 20th Century.

The Ancient Egyptians was the first known pottery makers. The Romans also created pottery in great number for utilitarian purposes. However, it is the Ancient Chinese who invented porcelain, in 500 AD. Ancient pottery antiques are usually kept in museums.

Earthenware was the most prevalent type of pottery during the 17th century. 17th Century ceramics was started by a group of farmers in Burslem who simply wanted to develop something to make butter easier to sell. They utilized a great variety of clay and coal in the area to create pots.

The West has been attempting to copy Chinese-made porcelain to no avail – that is, until the 18th century. Ehrenfried Tschirnhaus of the Meissen factory successfully imitated the Chinese porcelain. Europe's porcelain competed with Chinese porcelain. By this time, refined white pots are already cheap and are very common among European bourgeoisie.

During the 19th century, there was a big decline on the quality of ceramics due to the industrial revolution. This was because ceramics were already being made mechanically; only a few were still made by hand. Ceramics became indistinguishable from each other. It seemed like their cultural and aesthetic values have been replaced by a purely utilitarian worth. As a result, there has been a backlash on the quality of ceramics produced.

During the 20th century, notable artists (such as Pablo Picasso) emerged. He created beautiful and noteworthy vases and pieces that until now are very popular with art collectors.

Potteries can also be classified according to their manufacturers. Here is a list of some notable manufacturers: Grueby pottery, McCoy Pottery, Meissen porcelain, Metlox Pottery, Moorcroft Pottery, Rookwood pottery, and Wedgwood.

Other pottery manufacturers include: Zsolnay Porcelain, Zaalberg Pottery, W.S. George Pottery Company, W. H. Grindley & Co. Ltd. Pottery, W. J. Gordy Pottery, Weller Pottery, Villeroy and Boch Ceramics, Tuscan Decoro Pottery, and Alfred Meakin Ltd pottery.

**Furniture**

Furniture is probably the most varied and the most sought-after kind of antique. Pieces of furniture are not merely functional as they can also be used for decorative and ornamental purposes. Chairs, tables, desks, sofas, dressers, mirrors, cabinets, chests, bookcases, benches, and footstools – all fall into the category of furniture. As an aspiring collector, you must understand that furniture can be best classified according to the period where they came from.

The political, cultural, and artistic mindset of the people belonging to a particular era usually reflects the designs of their furniture. Also, pieces of furniture from the same period also tend to have similar themes and designs.

The following are the significant classes of furniture design: Art Deco (characterized by bold geometric shapes), Art Nouveau (floral designs made of iron), Arts and Crafts (1860 – 1910), Baroque (characterized by heavy moldings and twisted columns, both of which reflect grandeur and sophistication), Bauhaus (influenced by the designer William Morris who mainly used steel), Chippendale (influenced by Thomas Chippendale), Colonial (influenced by patriotism to one's mother country), Danish Modern (clean lines, and simple forms), Depression-era (influenced by the great depression during the 1920s-1940s; the materials used are cheap, such as low-quality wood), Early American (1608 – 1720), Federal (characterized by federal motifs, such as the eagle), French-style Furniture (lavish and flamboyant), Gothic (12th century), Queen Anne (also known as "late baroque"), Renaissance (classic proportions and arches), Retro, Rococo, Shaker (simple and functional),and Victorian.

Popular designers of furniture are Thomas Chippendale, Gustav Stickley, and Charles and Ray Eames.

**Jewelry**

There are different types of jewelry: rings, necklaces, brooches, earrings, cufflinks, and bracelets. They can be made of any material but the ones with high market value are usually made of gold, silver, and diamond. Pieces of jewelry can also be classified according to the era where they came from: Ancient Greek, Roman, Middle Ages, Renaissance, 18th Century, and 19th Century.

## Paintings, Sculptures, Photography, and Music

The first instances of recognizable art were traced back to Mesopotamia and Ancient Egypt. However, antique collections can be divided into six categories: Medieval art (200 – 1430), Renaissance art (1300 – 1602), Neoclassicism (1602 – 1830), Romanticism (1790 – 1880), Modern art (1900 – 1970), and Contemporary art (1960s – present day).

# Chapter 3: Notable Antiques & Antique Experts

If you will be invited to a dinner party exclusively for antique collectors and buyers, it would be very advantageous if you have basic knowledge of the most expensive and the most prominent paintings, sculptures, furniture, and jewelry! If you do know your history, it would save you the trouble of Googling everything during every antique-related social gathering. Besides, by showing other enthusiasts that you're quite knowledgeable about the world of antiques, they'll be encouraged to have deals with you.

**Paintings & Sculptures**

The following are the most valuable paintings and artworks in the whole world: Eight Elvises by Andy Warhol ($100.9 million), 1967 Self Portrait By Andy Warhol (£10,793,250), Portrait of Adele Bloch Bauer I by Gustav Klimt ($135), Portrait of Adele Bloch Bauer II by Gustav Klimt ($88), No.5, 1948 by Jackson Pollock ($140), Diana and Actaeon by Titian

(£50), Dora Maar au Chat by Pablo Picasso ($95,216,000), Garcon a la Pipe by Pablo Picasso (£58 million), Triptych, 1976 by Francis Bacon($86.3), Nude, Green Leaves and Bust by Pablo Picasso ($106.5 million), Woman III by Willem de Kooning ($137.5 million), Andy Warhol's self portrait, Modern Rome by Joseph William Turner (£28,860,000), L'Homme Qui Marche (Walking Man I) (£65 million), and lastly, The Mona Lisa by Leonardo da Vinci ($713m).

## More Detail for the Curious

Aren't you a bit curious about some of the pieces mentioned above? Well, these facts should partly satisfy your curiosity:

- ❖ Eight Elvises (1963) is a 12-foot-long silkscreen painting which was sold in 2008 for more than 100 million dollars. It is the eleventh most valuable painting in the world. Its current value is $100.9m.

- 1967 is simply a self-portrait of Andy Warhol. It is one of the eleven paintings that were produced by the artist. It features his signature pose—with his hand to his mouth. On 2011, his painting was sold in London by Christie's for £10,793,250.

- Portrait of Adele Bloch-Bauer I is a 1907 painting by Austrian symbolist painter, Gustav Klimt. It is the world's third most expensive painting and was sold in 2006 to Ronald Lauder for US$135 million. There are rumors that Klimt had a romantic relationship with the subject of the painting, Adele Block Bauer. The painting measures 138 x 138 cm. What makes the painting valuable more than its aesthetic beauty is the story behind it. Adele Block-Bauer, being a Jew was forced to leave Austria. The Nazis confiscated the painting. For more than 60 years it has been displayed in a gallery in Vienna. But it was returned to Adele's niece in 2010.

- Portrait of Adele Bloch-Bauer II is Gustav Klimt's second work. Its market value is $88 million, currently it is the 13th most valuable painting.

- No. 5, 1948 is an 8' x 4' abstract painting of Jackson Pollock. It also inspired the emergence of abstract expressionism. His piece features Pollock's famous technique – drip-and-pour. In fact, Time Magazine even called him "Jack the Dripper" because of his one-of-a-kind painting style. It was rumored to be the most expensive painting when it was sold to David Geffen for approximately $140m.

- Water Lilies (also called Nympheas) by Claude Monet (1840 – 1926) are one of the most famous Impressionist works of art in the 19th century. It portrays Monet's flower garden which has become his subject during his last 30 years. Monet used oil painting in his masterpiece. On June 19, 2007, one of Monet's paintings in this collection sold for £18.5. On June 24, 2008, another painting (also from this collection) sold for £41 million.

❖ Mona Lisa is Leonardo da Vinci's famous work. Even today, it is the most valuable painting in the world. It features a mysterious smiling woman as its subject. It used sfumato and chiaroscuro – two painting techniques in which Leonardo was considered to be unparalleled.

**Well-Known Collectors**

Famous art collectors are the following: Roman Abramovich, Mary Boone, Steven Cohen, David Geffen, Henry Kravis, Leonard and Ronald Lauder, Andrew Lloyd Webber, Stavros Niarchos, Edward G. Robinson, Charles Saatchi, and Steven Spielberg.

**Antique Experts**

The following people are the most notable antique experts: Alastair Dickenson, Andew Nebbett, Del Mar Antique Show, Harvey Withers, Helaine Fendelman, Henry Sandon, Michael Hogben, and Yosef Goldman.

# Chapter 4: Hunting Antiques

What makes the antiques business different from other "normal" businesses is that the former is highly unregulated. There is no financial services compensation scheme if anything goes wrong with your transaction. Pieces cannot be easily liquidated because they have very few buyers and sometimes, offers can be very hard to come by. If you want to invest on antique collections, you may want to consider taking expert advice on what kinds of antiques would "come in flavor" for the next ten years.

Here are some tips that would help newbie art collectors/investors in looking for investments:

First, only buy from established, preferably famous, antique dealers. If you want to make sure that your money won't go to waste, only transact with members of famous trade associations in your country. Research their credibility. Before you put your money on something, make sure that it's the "real deal" first.

Second, look for original and untouched antique. The best investments are those antiques that haven't been restored yet. If you do not have the budget, you can simply buy little pieces that usually cost £5,000. Those would be good decade-long investments.

Third, only buy from famous, big-name jewelry designers such as Van Cleef & Arpels or Tiffany, if you can afford it. Instead of buying what is popular now, think of what would be popular ten years from now. Antiques and jewelries, much like clothes, come in and out of fashion. Invest based on your gut.

Fourth, as much as possible, buy the rarest items or the most valuable. Sometimes, it would be best if you invest on something unique or unusual. You have to look for an edge – something you won't find in most other antiques. Ask yourself the following questions: What makes this piece special? What makes it unique from all the rest? Does its quality justify its price?

Fifth, beware of fraud and watch out for visible, physical signs that the piece has been restored. If your gut tells you the piece is a forgery, resist your desire of wanting to buy it until you have confirmation that it is authentic. Proof of authenticity, like historic information and lineage of ownership, always increase the market value of the antique because it somehow gives the piece a strong sense of "personality." Look for items that are either signed by a well-known person or have unique markings. Signatures and markings add to a piece's authenticity.

Sixth, be aware of laws and regulations. Countries have laws implemented to protect their cultural heritage. There are particular types of art and antiquities that are restricted from being exported, imported, or sold to other people. The government of the country involved could simply confiscate the item with no compensation to the owner.

Where does one hunt for antiques? There are very famous international art affairs wherein an investor could start hunting for pieces:

American International Fine Art Fair, Dallas Art Fair, PrintBasel (International Fine Print Fair), Art International Zurich, Art Toronto (Toronto International Art Fair), and Royal Dublin Society Art Fair. Auction houses are also highly recommended. They include: Asian Art auction Alliance Co., Ltd., Asian Auction Week (AAW), Casa d'Aste VIP, Capitoliumart Casa D'Aste, Borobudur Chinese Contemporary Auction.

# Chapter 5: Earning Bucks from Antiquing

Are you itching to know how to sell the works you've collected? Well, by keeping these pointers and facts in mind, you should be able to make money without having to worry about confusion and losses:

One common mistake that people usually commit in relation to antiques is acquiring little knowledge on what they already have. Some people are surprised to know that the piece that they have sold to an antique dealer for such a cheap price is actually extremely expensive. So, the trick is you should not rely on your buyer in knowing the market value of your piece. Do not let anyone take advantage of you and the best way to do that is to remain informed about the value of the object that you are trying to sell.

You have to do your research beforehand. You have to know how much it is worth. Evaluate the condition of your item because that will have a big impact on its commercial value. There are 12 factors that could affect the market value of an item: age, condition, beauty, design, size, and historical value, locality of origin, demand, rarity, uniqueness, category, and individuality. Note that even if your piece excels in one factor, it does not necessarily mean that you can sell it for a high price. It is the combination of these factors that determines its commercial value. You can also try studying price guides in eBay auctions, recent sales, and printed advertisements.

On the other hand, if you are trying to buy antiques (to sell your shop), you have to have previous knowledge on the item that you are going to buy. But more than that, you also have to follow your gut feeling. If you think that the piece that you found is quite interesting or has unique aesthetic value that sets it apart, there is also a possibility that other people might also find it interesting. The ability to sort out valuable gems from piles of junk is one acquired talent that a good collector must have. If you do not have it yet, after years and years of practice in the field of collecting antiques, you will.

If you are selling your item to an antique dealer, expect to receive 25-50 percent of the original price. Do not be surprised if you will only get that amount. You have to understand that it might take months or years to look for a customer willing to pay good money for the piece.

Frankly state your price at the starting point of negotiation. Keep the price a little higher than what you have in mind to know how high the dealer is willing to go. You might get lucky and your dealer will take it at the price you want.

If you're antique has sentimental value, especially if it is a family heirloom, think really hard before you sell it. And when you do, don't ever look back. Move on. You have to consider the fact that there is a big chance that you will not get it back. The dealer is not obliged to sell it back to you once you have sold it to him.

What are your options? What could be your medium of communication with your buyers?

## Online

What makes online selling advantageous compared to opening an antique store, doing yard sales, or selling your items to a dealer? Compared to opening an antique store, it is inexpensive to get started; online selling platforms give statistics which can be very helpful in terms of answering questions like "What's hot?" There is also no commission, only charges! When selling online though, be sure to take great pictures and give complete, honest, and accurate descriptions, which include historical data and if possible, a list of previous owners. You also have to provide detailed descriptions regarding the flaws of the pieces; if there is any damage or stain, you should say so. It is better to be honest than have the item returned to you. Remember, if an item is sold, immediately remove your advertisement. If you are looking for a great website to start with, try Ruby Lane, Oodle, or eBay.

## Yard Sales

Consider placing an ad in your local news paper or post an advertisement online that you will be having a garage sale of antique items.

This way, you would be able to attract possible buyers and antique enthusiasts. In displaying things, you should put similar things together. Pictures, paintings, and sculptures should be arranged together. Books and maps should be in the same table; pottery and ceramics should be displayed together as well. Print out historical descriptions and other necessary details to pick your potential buyers' curiosity.

## Antique Store

If you are planning to open an antique store, you have to consider the exact location of your store. As much as possible, you should open your store in a place where there are many people. Because the antiques business is not really booming, you have to make sure that your rent is not too high. Otherwise you might need to close your business and declare bankruptcy before you even make a sale. Information dissemination is very important, using the Internet as a communication platform is an inexpensive way to get in touch with possible costumers and buyers.

# Chapter 6: Taking Care of Antiques

One of the most commonly asked question in the trade of antiquing is, "How do experts take care of the pieces they collect?" Even though your aim is to buy and sell antiques, you should learn the answer to that question – after all, you're going to have to care for the pieces you've bought for quite some time. Well, here are some tips that should serve as good answers:

**Furniture Care**

For antiques with original finish, avoid environments with extreme temperature or humidity because they only accelerate the deterioration of the finish. If you are living with children, do not place glassware on surfaces without mat protection. In terms of cleaning, you can either use a vacuum cleaner or the traditional soft cloth. The cloth should be mildly dampened with solvent-based cleaning wax to clean the surface and remove dust. After dust is removed, immediately wipe it with dry paper towels. Do not use polishes or spray waxes on the pieces because doing so could possibly destroy their value.

In terms of positioning them in a room, furniture should be at least three feet away from any heat source (radiator or heater) and never directly in front of it. If you have the budget, it is also good to invest in a humidifier in order to regulate the humidity in the room, especially during winter season. The optimum, non-damaging humidity is usually 50-55% relative humidity.

In terms of dealing with woodworm, which usually appear in late spring (June or May), make sure that you buy the right insecticide or any woodworm treatment. But use it only on unfinished surfaces because the fluid might damage the paintwork. Also, warm air is a very effective alternative.

**Paintings**

Like furniture, paintings are very vulnerable to fluctuations in temperature and humidity, as well as to insect attacks. This is why it is important to have regular checks on your paintings (both front and back) because early detection and correction can minimize the damage. Do not attempt to go the DIY route. Seek help from a professional. The optimum level of relative humidity is 50-60% and the ideal temperature is 20-22 degrees Celsius. Paintings should never be photocopied.

**Pottery & Porcelain**

As much as possible, valuable pottery and porcelain should be kept behind glass, undisturbed and dust-free. In terms of cleaning, a soft sponge with a dash of liquid soap should be used. After cleaning, use a fine linen glass cloth and a hairdryer to dry the pieces.

**Security**

There are security companies, such as Chubb or Banham, that offer alarms and locks. You can also consult the local Crime Prevention Officer of the local police. You should always expect the worst, only then will you prevent it from happening. The police's efforts are usually hindered in recovering stolen property because owners are unable to provide photographs and descriptions of the pieces. Recovery agencies, such as Art Loss Register, could only try to return stolen pieces if they know what they are looking for. When taking pictures, it is best to use a digital camera and avoid reflections. Save your images in your email or in a memory stick.

# Chapter 7: How to Acquire the Best Antiques at a Great Price

Antiques can be really expensive because of their quality, rarity, and old age. Antique pieces are made of high quality materials that last for a long time. Most of them are also difficult to find. These factors contribute to the antiques' expensive price tag. What you need to do is find ways that can help you acquire the best antiques at a great price.

Here are some great tips and ideas:

**Know where to find cheap antiques**

Sometimes, all you need to do is to find the right place where you can find cheap antiques. There are a number of places where you can find great deals for antique pieces.

1. *Sales at private homes*

This includes estate sales, garage sales, or yard sales. You can find great prices from these sales because people are trying to dispose off their things as fast as possible. They are more willing to lower their prices. And sometimes, these people do not know that they are selling something valuable. They do not know that the item they are selling for a few dollars is an antique worth thousands of dollars. There are a lot of stories of people who found antiques in yard or garage sales at a very low price because the owner does not know its value. People who hold yard sales often post their events online so be sure to check websites like Craigslist, estatesales.net, and other websites for classified ads. You can even find a map of yard sale events in your area.

The only disadvantage of searching for antiques in these places is that you have to sift through a lot of piles and visit several sales in your area. This is because these sales do not only sell antiques but other stuff and junks as well. If you want to have a better chance at finding antiques in private home sales, you should consider checking out those sales held by people in your area who are known to collect antiques or who belong in an old family in your area and live in an ancestral house. They will most likely have antiques for sale.

## 2. *Thrift shops*

You can also find great antique pieces in thrift shops if you are really lucky. You can also check out charity thrift shops that hold sales and offer great prices for their items. Charity thrift shops sell items donated by people, which makes them more willing to offer their items at a lower price because they did not spend any money as their starting capital. The main purpose of this is to raise funds for their cause. You can find antiques in these places because the items for sale are usually donated by well-to-do families.

## 3. *Auctions*

You can get pretty decent prices for antiques at auctions. You can get an antique worth thousands of dollars for just a couple of hundred of dollars. This happens when you are the only one who bids for the antique or there are very few people who are interested in it. Just keep in mind that when you place your bid, there is no turning back. Do not place your bid just to increase the price of the antique for others. It could backfire and you would end up paying for something you do not really have. Or you might end up in trouble if you place a bid and you win but you do not have the money to back up your bid.

## 4. *Flea markets*

Art and antique suppliers usually gather at flea market to sell their stuff. The prices of antiques at these events are slightly higher than those of the prices at yard sales but you have more great choices because of the various sellers who participated in the event. The prices are slightly lower than in regular antique shops because flea markets intend to make quick sales.

## 5. *Online*

You can find really rare (and if you're lucky, cheap!) antique from websites such as eBay or Craigslist. There are antique dealers who sell their stuff online and there are also private collectors who are selling their stuff or are willing to swap in exchange for another antique. Just remember not to buy any large furniture online that has to be shipped because the shipping fee would be expensive. You should also be cautious because there are a lot of scammers online.

## Boost your negotiating skills

You should also need to boost your negotiating skills if you want to get great prices when buying antiques. Antique sellers and dealers are usually willing to lower their prices in certain situations. Here are some tips.

### 1. *Buy more than one*

Antique sellers are more willing to reduce their price if you are going to buy more than one item from them. Sellers like it when customers buy more than one item because it means more sales at a shorter period of time. They will find it difficult to turn down a wonderful customer like you when you ask for a discount because you are buying two or more from them which means a great sale for them even with the discount. They will also think that you might become a regular customer and bring some friends along if they give you a discount.

### 2. *Offer a lower price even if the price is good*

You should also try to offer a lower price even if you know that the antique is already a steal. Go up to the dealer and put on a deadpan expression. Do not gush about how cheap their products because you want to get a lower price, not make them increase their prices in the future.

You can start with questions like " Is this your best price for this piece?" or "May I make an offer for this piece?" You should then provide your price and if the seller responds with a higher price than your offer but lower than the original price of the piece, it means that he is willing to reduce the original price. You can then go back and forth until you have settled on a price.

### 3. *Point out flaws*

This is a tried and tested approach to negotiating a lower price. Look for a cut, a chip, a crack, or any damage that can potentially lower the price. If the damage is too obvious, like the broken leg of a chair or a missing part, there is no need to point it out to the seller because he already knows this and he already probably reduced the price for the damage. You will only get off on a bad start if you do this.

### 4. *Always be polite*

Some people think that intimidating the seller might get them a lower price. This is not a great idea because people are less willing to agree to your offer if you are antagonistic. What you can do is to kill them with kindness. When you make an offer, always put a smile on your face. You should also ask politely, even if you are pointing out a damage. This will give you a better chance at asking for a discount the next time you come back to the shop.

### 5. *Look for odd and unwanted pieces*

Antique shops often have pieces that they really want to get rid of and are willing to accept almost any price offer. You can usually find these items at the back of the shop, collecting dust and spider webs. Examples of these items are artworks with weird and sometimes creepy subjects or an odd piece that is a part of a large collection. You might just find what you are looking for if you sift through the odd pile and you might even get a great deal for it.

## 6. Negotiate for other stuff

Aside from the antique, you should also consider negotiating with other things involving the sale such as the shipping, repairs, cleaning, installation, documentations, and so on. For example, if you bought an antique wardrobe that costs thousands of dollars, you can ask the dealer if you can get free delivery for it. The dealer will be more motivated to say yes because you are a valued customer who just bought one of his most expensive items. If you bought a chandelier, you can also ask for free installation. You may not get a discount for the antique itself but you can still get a great deal by negotiating for other stuff involving the sale.

# Conclusion

Thank you again for purchasing this book!

I hope this book was able to help you broaden your understanding of the world of antiques. If you've read everything in this book carefully, you should be able to pinpoint the finest pieces. You should also have enough knowledge in buying, selling, and protecting antiques.

The next step is to start learning from firsthand experience. There's no need to be afraid of closing not-so-impressive deals during your first few tries – everyone starts somewhere, even the greatest art aficionados.

Finally, if you enjoyed this book, then I'd like to ask you for a favor, would you be kind enough to leave a review for this book on Amazon? It'd be greatly appreciated!

Thank you and good luck!

Printed in Great Britain
by Amazon